kestrel

sparrow

butterfly

lizard

crab

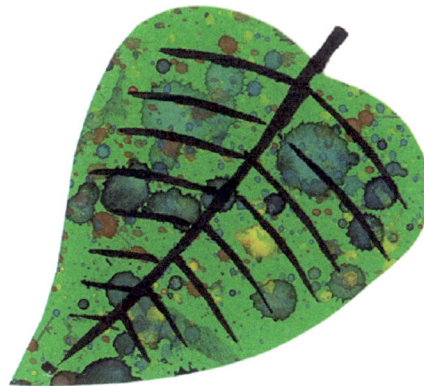

leaf

kingfisher

acorn

mouse

toadstool

terrapin

flower

The bird on the cover of this book is a redwing.

This book belongs to

....

b small

Published by b small publishing ltd.
www.bsmall.co.uk
© b small publishing ltd. 2024

1 2 3 4 5

Printed in China by WKT Co. Ltd. on FSC-certified paper, supporting responsible forestry.

Editorial: Sam Hutchinson
Art director: Vicky Barker
Design: Louise Millar & Christian Francis

ISBN 978-1-916851-19-1

British Library Cataloguing-in-Publication Data.
A catalogue record for this book is available from the British Library.

A MOMENT IN NATURE

CLARE BEATON

b small

River

The river slowly flows through the fields, full of little fish that the kingfisher and heron try to catch. The frog had better watch out as herons eat them, too!

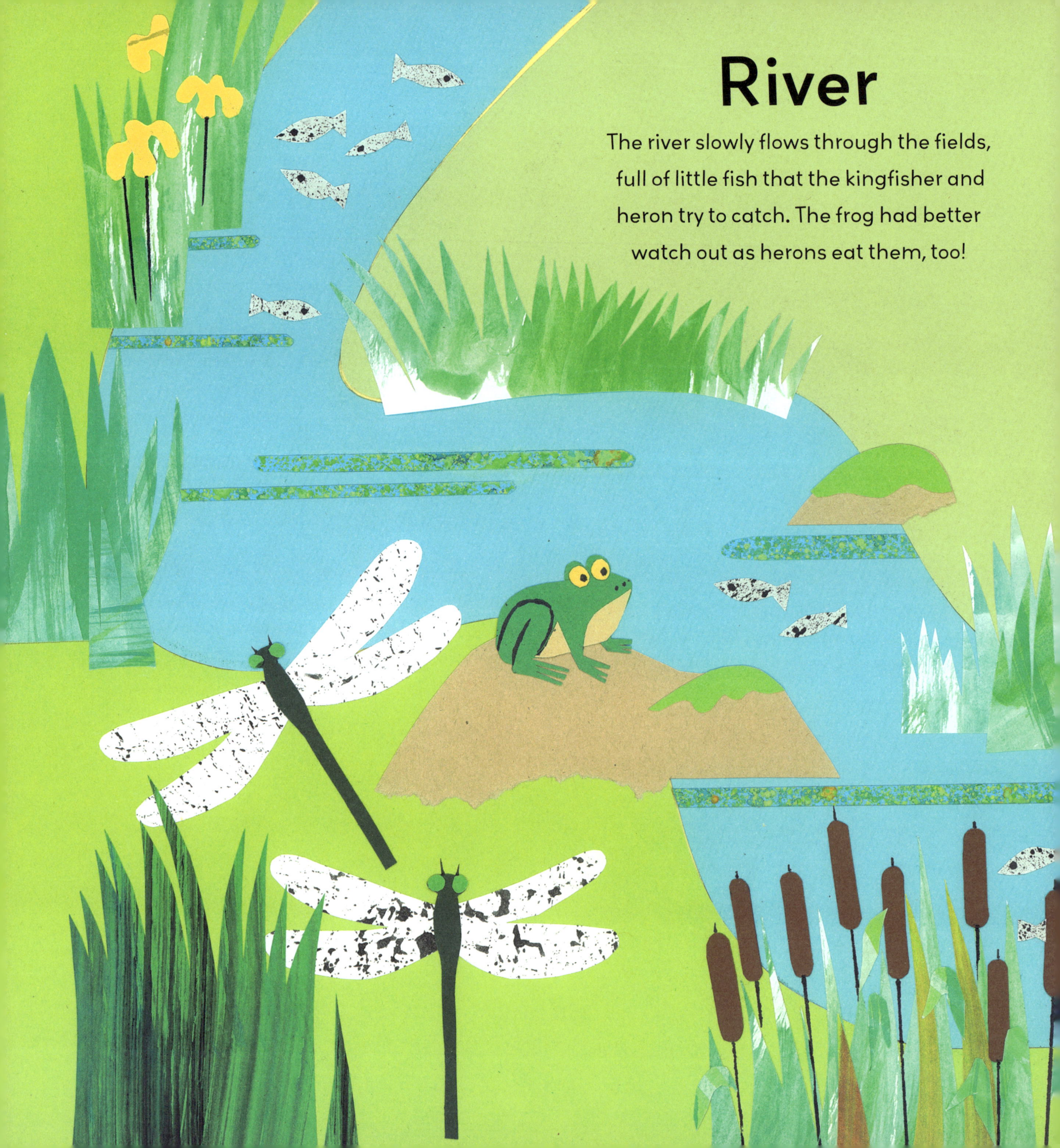

Field

Two donkeys share a field with some horses.
Autumn is coming, and the leaves are beginning to
change colour from green to yellow, orange and red.
The hedge is full of different berries.

Beach

Many things wash up at the edge of the waves –
pebbles, seaweed, and pretty shells of all shapes
and colours. A pair of knots are searching for
something to eat.

Allotment

You can grow your own delicious vegetables and fruit on an
allotment, in a garden or even in a flowerpot. It's so exciting,
especially when it is time to pick and eat them!
Which things here do you like to eat?

Winter

On a cold, snowy day, a red squirrel has left its drey to go exploring. A blackbird is eating holly berries. Other birds, such as seedeaters, struggle to find much to eat in the winter. A bird feeder is a real lifesaver!

Woodland

Lots of insects and small creatures live in the leaf mould and fungi, which lie under the trees. A fox trots silently through the wood towards its den, also known as an earth.

Coastal cliffs

High up on the coastal cliffs lives a colony of puffins.
One has caught some tiny fish to eat.

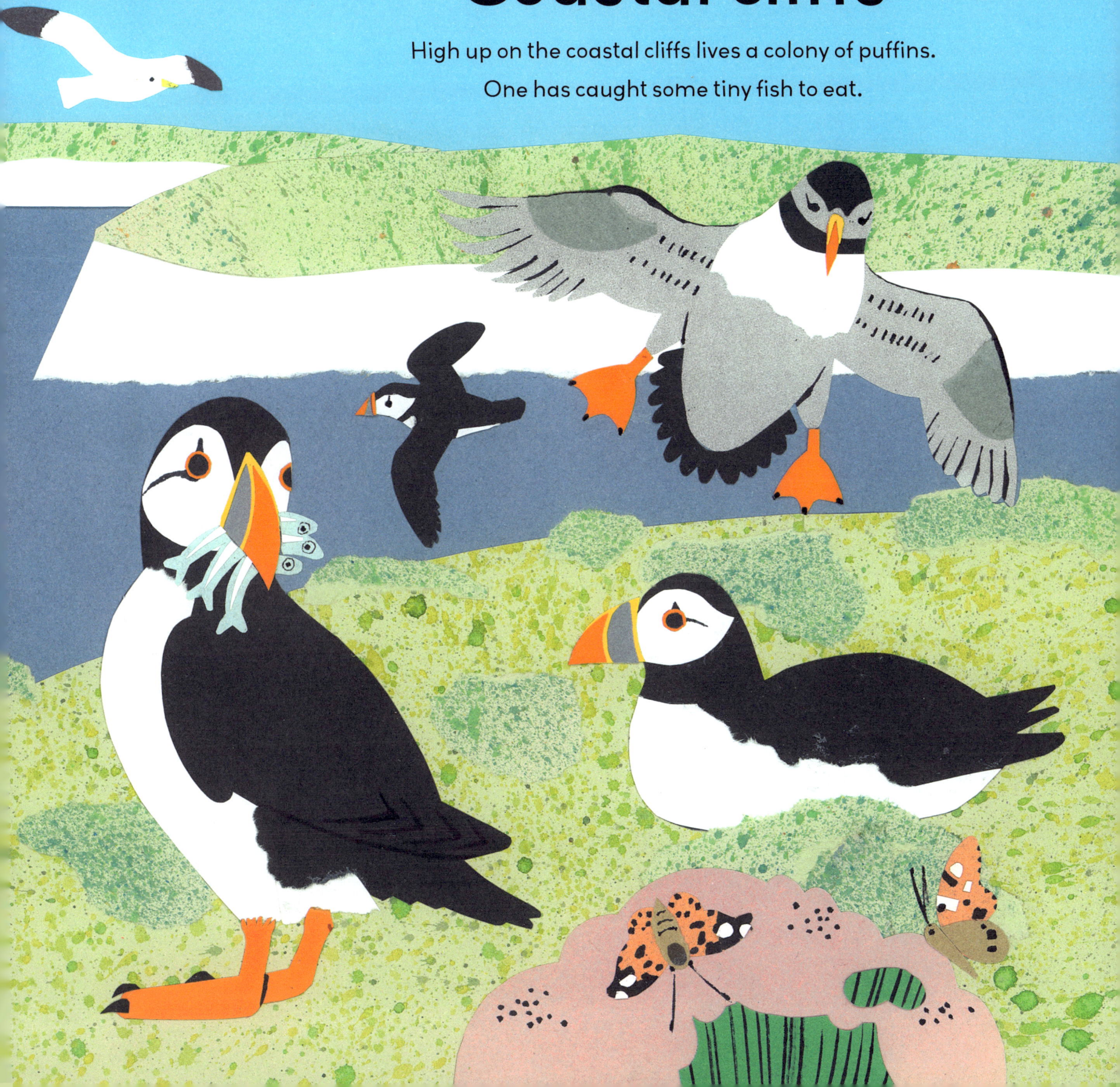

Spring

After the winter, everything starts to wake up.
The birch is covered in catkins as the first leaves appear.
There are wildflowers in the meadow, and rabbits
nibble the fresh, new grass.

Night

As the moon and stars appear, nocturnal creatures emerge. Bats flit this way and that, and the light from a lantern attracts moths. A family of owls looks down from the branch of a tree.

Garden pots

Colourful flowers attract butterflies and bees to the garden.
The first shoots start to appear in some pots. But beware
of slugs and snails, who will also be attracted
to all these!

Rock pools

The tide has gone out, leaving beautiful rock pools full of small sea creatures. Now is the time for oystercatchers and other wading birds to feed on crustaceans before they disappear again under the waves.

Forest

Conifers are covered in needles instead of leaves, and the fir cones contain seeds.
A tiny firecrest pecks at an insect on one fir cone. Far below, a group of deer comes
out to graze in a clearing while a buzzard soars high overhead on a thermal.

Nest

Adult birds make hundreds of trips collecting
insects and worms to feed their young.
When the fledglings are old enough,
they will fly the nest and feed themselves.

Underwater

The pond is teeming with life. Among the many water plants live a frog, water beetles, snails and other creatures. Can you see the newt? It is amphibious – hibernating on land in the winter and living in water the rest of the year.

Autumn

The sun is setting on an autumn day.
The yellow and orange leaves are falling.
A kestrel hovers in the sky – it has
spotted something it's hoping to catch!

City

Lots of wild creatures live in towns and cities. Scavengers such
as rats, pigeons and foxes feed on food discarded by humans.
The pigeon eating a chip under the statue better take care!

Farm

Chickens and their chicks forage for insects and seeds to eat. They lay their eggs anywhere.
The cockerel is perched up in the pear tree, which has attracted lots of wasps.
They like to eat the ripe fruit.

Mountains

A ram with large, curling horns looks over the
dry stone wall. The wall is covered in moss and
lichens, which is a sign of clean, damp air.
A lizard and a slow worm bask in the sunshine.

Park

A goose, some swans and a family
of ducks are swimming in the pond.
After the rain, there are puddles to enjoy too.

There are over twenty different birds in this book, along with lots of kinds of fish, butterflies and other creatures. But there is only ONE stag beetle, ONE red squirrel, ONE spider, ONE ladybird and ONE shrimp. Can you find each of them?

stag beetle

red squirrel

spider

shrimp

ladybird

How many moths are there on the **NIGHT** page?

How many pigeons are there on the **CITY** page?

How many rabbits are there on the **SPRING** page?

How many limpets are there on the **ROCK POOLS** page?

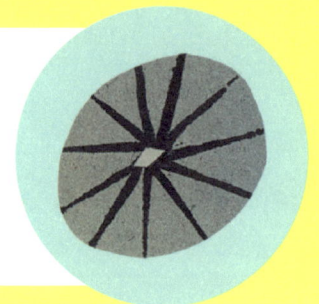

Now for one last challenge! There is an ant hiding on every page – can you find it?

NATURE WORDS

Amphibious

Living both on land and in water.

Colony

A group of animals of the same kind, all living close together.

Crustaceans

A group of living things that includes crabs, lobsters and shrimps.

Drey

A squirrel's nest.

Fledgling

A young bird that has grown feathers and is learning to fly.

Foraging

Looking in nature for things to eat and use.

Fungi

A group of living things that includes mushrooms and toadstools.

Grazing

Feeding on grass.

Hibernating

Spending all winter in an inactive, sleep-like state.

Knots

Wading birds that feed along the shore.

Scavengers

Creatures feeding on discarded things or other animals that are already dead.

Thermal

A current of warm air.

puffin

wasp

bat

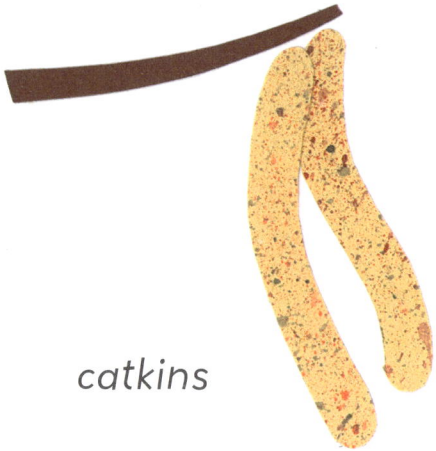

catkins

tomato

newt

snowflake

frog

slow worm

starfish

snail

fish

duck

fir cone